Aero Travel Inno

I0019603

Computer Guide & Aero Technical Business

By: Zac Oleynik

It is early in the morning and an aerocraft is landing on a grassy field. They decided to land by a laboratory and in the sky across the traffic orange electric line ball weights can be seen. The weather is kind of foggy and some military humvees can be seen driving on the road to the laboratory. Their would be a young Scientist with small dark gray square rim glasses wearing a gray and dark gray shirt and dark blue jeans. Wearing lab work shoes. The workers would stand around him and a patient would sit with its bare Caucasian chest facing into the room. The treatment for diseases of cancer is now ready for you all to see and observe. The method we will be using is done by oxygen distribution through the body to the cells and you all will notice is that it gets rid of cancer in the cells. Another client mentions it stops the replication of cancer cells in the body. The workers standing by greatly and incredibly liked the ideas. The man would be known as Sergei and a leading guy in the treatment and detailing of the elimination of cancers and diseases in the body. He would close his file folders and place them in the drawer on the table.

The men and ladies stood around the table in the room and the men and ladies told the person his shirt set on the table that he can put his shirt back on. Sergei would thank the men and ladies for showing up and he would join them and they would turn the lights off in the laboratory and follow each other down a hall and out a door to the humvees in the parking places. He would get in with some of the guys and they would give him a ride to the military base. Sergei and the men would go to a reception place and would begin to prepare publication material for treatment purposes. He would meet and talk to this man and share and introduce to him his business and later in the day have him on the radio. Welcome Sergei, Zac would welcome him as he opens the door and shows him into a luxury apartment. The room would be kind of dark and would be very clean. Their would be a sofa in the room, a large dresser across from it and art pieces by a famed artist Shlevko who was known for making figurines and décor eggs. He would also paint landscapes and themes such as the two women in a canoe on a lake by their friends home. They would be dressed in dresses of purple and blue and would be wearing thin coat like hats on their heads to refrain from Sun burn. The important part of his portraits were how well they were made and designed. Zac had his own jewelry business and would grade, weigh and put on presentation stones made in the earth and cultivated through digging and mining process.

He would show Sergei the products available forsale. Zac would make newer products and would share with Sergei the sun dial wrist watches and the sun dial clocks with Amethyst stones for the outer dial on the sun dial clocks and Amethyst stones on the face of the gold Aucer clocks. The wrist watches would be of leather straps, gold aucer body, using a wood pole on it and would have Amethysts on it. There would be additional products of gold aucer mushrooms and a gold aucer aquarium. The sun dials were designed to be indian with stones that come from the planet. Jewelry of bracelets would also be assembled. The bracelets would consist of barrel clasps, sterling silver wire, and aucer beads and stones of Amethysts. Zac would design stones and assemble citrine and turquoise also. Zac walked to his house and went to his company building and decided to lay on his neighbors bed and write about broadcasting on the radio and selling programming to the businesses. After typing the brochure he decided to search for some shops and businesses near him and have them get a copy of the emails.

The company of robots worked on the early designs of an electromagnetic sender and receiver for music broadcasting all around and the research of whether or not the signals could be sent all around the planet and through outerspace. As well as searching the skies and receiving the source of lights from the stars and converting it to electronic audio. The process of potentially obtaining content from extraterrestrial persons from space on other planets in space. Where most and many forms of the technology and Science is based and built on electro magnetic technologies. On some planets here are human beings that work, go to the school and go interact with people and have fun and enjoy nature animals and life. He would explain his new product of the gold aucer. The aucer would be made from clays of either terracotta or a gray and would be shaped into bars up to a pound and many ounces. They would be grooved by etching the lines around the sides and scraping them into place and then the bars would be stamped with a unique serial number that would be recorded. Each piece would be placed on an oven tray to be baked. The nuggets and the decorating eggs. Would be crafted the same and the nuggets would be shaped like a poultry nugget with a flat base and the side and top around the design would be etched. The front would be stamped. After they would be oven baked they would be placed to cool. They would later be painted with several brushes by hand. This would be done by mixing gold paint, glitter glue and setting stones to the front of the aucers. Eventually plates, cups, and bowls would be made the same. There could be glaze used to give it a glass covering for use for many purposes. There would be the design of Amethyst coated with glitter glue with option of glaze finish. There would be the design of gold paint, Amethyst, and glitter glue with option of a glaze finish. The stones coating choices of citrine, turquoise, sapphire, amethyst, and many more made brilliant designs. There would also be bills for stores with the design printed by stones as the ink.

When the products and designs are complete the serial numbers would be registered and a authenticity form would be made and would contain the details about the items. They would then be placed on display. Typically a red or black crushed velvet. It would be quite sparkly and be of praise of some natives of the land. Which had quite a role in the ideas of production and sales. Zac would begin by showing to him the broadcasting room and he would see there would be digital media players, the broadcaster and a video tape player. He and Sergei could notice how the video tape played and the music could be heard through the speakers near the broadcaster. When Sergei seen this style of programming he would be fascinated and impressed by the ideas of programming. Were live now, here in the station today I have Sergei as a guest and I would like to introduce him to the listeners here. --And Cut-- As he turns the music down. First begin by introducing yourself. Hi my name is Sergei and I work as a chemical biologist technician at the laboratories here in the city. We have many departments and we specialize in electrical engineering. We install series of line balls that are about the size of a basketball to keep electrical cables and communication cables from swaying and breaking along the roads. They are colored balls that attach along the electric and communication lines and are commonly of an orange color. Many travellers, kids, teens and adults find these astonishing and awesome to observe as a rarity across the country and around the planet. We had a story about a what if; there was a family related to everybody on the planet. It would be obvious that the military and Government would be highly interested and they would go after them to capture them, because they would be related to everyone on the planet by blood and genetic life. Here they would seen send suburbans, humvees from the military and tanks well as people that enforce the law. Zac commented I go to the restaurants all the time, chatting about this and I'm sure I'm not the only one that finds this stuff impressive. Sergei yeah I find it fascinating. At the laboratories we came up with a method to reduce cancer and the spread and growth of cancer. We discussed how oxygen can be used and delivered to the cells throughout the entire body and this affect reduces the growth and spread of cancer by stopping and reducing and eliminating the cancers in the cells because of additional factors like the change in the ph of the body. The oxygen treatment by oral mouth capsules can therefore eliminate cancer. Sergei tell us about other projects you work on. This can make males like females and females like males and both genders. The males and both genders. The males can be both males and females and females the option of being male and female by body mechanics and exercise at the home, office and gym. Sergei that is many topics to discuss today and thanks great listeners for enjoying our programming here we will begin this hour with rock and roll and classical heavy electric guitar music.

Presto lets get to the music programming now. He pressed play on the video tape player and returned the music on the broadcasting system. Thank you Sergei very much I would like to have you on the radio for the upcoming show. Here is your reservation for a motel room and some cash about $40.00. It appears great I will see you tomorrow. Zac walked him further to the door from the desk in the room where he got the envelope from a drawer. He showed the guy to the exit and he left. The broadcast station continued on and Zac got some fruits and some chilled coffee for the evening and thought to nap on the sofa. He began to focus on a card program and a software program that have an internet radio with a vumeter that is animated to the tones of the audio sound. The customers could play audio files and hear radio from around the planet and could add to it. The goals would be to make plenty of extra profit for commercial projects. Would they be considered foreign. Maybe but they could be great friends and sure they probably shop and there are probably Governments on those planets. They are all intellectual and there is many diverse people and they all have talents and many have characteristics. Typically people would expect technology like vehicles, Science, and aero space to be in perhaps electromagnetic achievements. In the deep mountains and forrests. The amazing and great foilage can be seen of many trees on the mountains. The green short grass, fluffy weeds, and the multi colored leafs. There would be great and alright roads that would go through the forrests of the deep mountains. During this time and the spring and summer months the weather would be great about seventy six to seventy four degrees Fahrenheit. There would be quite a bit of traffic but very few vehicles during the day and early evening. During the evening the sun can be seen through the moon to the city. It is early in the Summer and Shlevko meets Sergei and he has iced coffee and grape juice at Shlevko's house.

They enjoy the day and Sergei likes how Shlevko has a great beard and is dressed in a plait cotton shirt and blue jeans and short athletic cozy gray, dark gray and black sneakers. Sergei begins to tell Shlevko about the treatment break throughs of Volcom. Shlevko decides to help fund the projects and Sergei has some of his co-workers come and help setup the equipment. He has patients that were looking and researching to get remedies for the spread and decrease of cancer to work on this newer treatment method. Shlevko observes the display screen and two people; the patient and the friend, or assistant of the patient sit on the chairs in the work area and they are given two capsules and the option for an injection. They do both and Shlevko sees how the properties of the treatment in both the capsules and the injection, work by distributing its properties to all the cells of the body and decrease and diminish the spread of cancer by not only fixing optionally the ph or restore of the ph but by eliminating the cancers from the properties of the treatments. Shelevjo and Sergei are both happy and pleased with the treatments and Shlevko gets to some garden work outside. For this year he grew almost a complete yard of grapes for grape juice and wines. Him and some of his men that would help with his projects helped picking the grapes and placing them in a barrel as it began to get filled they would roll it over to a crate in the garage and would pour the grapes into the crate and the workers would continue loading the wheel barrel and filling the crate with the grapes.

When done Shlevko would show the men how to squeeze the grapes to large plastic dispensers and he would show them how to fill the bottles and place the lids and set them for sale to the customers. During the spring weather the wooded trees around the house of Shlevko had the appearance of dark green foilage. The water droplets on the trees had many colors that would sparkle on the water droplets. When the water would run off the foilage it would fall to the grass around the trees. He went to the side of his house and got his bucket and carried it across to the pond by his house and dipped it down in the water and filled it about 2/3 carried it by the garden by his yard and began to water the grapes that were growing there. There were about sixty to seventy pounds of grapes.

Each were of a fresh purple and green colors. He would grow the grapes for the month and would see if they were complete he would set more places to grow and plant more grapes during this time. Shlevko wanted to make grape juices for the stores and the markets in the city. It is about three thirty in the day and Shlevko decides to begin loading a cart on the rear of several horses with about fourty four bottles of grape juice. He would then travel to the markets and when he arrived he would meet with the clerks that would buy the merchandise for the stores. He would return with several workers from the during the time they got there they would help him clean and the perimeter and would assist in mowing the lawn, trimming grass and pouring fresh soil in the yard and planting the seeds by digging to the sides the dirt and placing the seeds and pushing the dirt back in place and smoothing it with a hand shovel. When the work was complete. Shlevko would pay the workers and offer them more work and he would provide them a ride to the city and go to work, travel, and camp around. Shlevko then began to pack brown paper bags with grapes for the markets in the city. He filled three bags and folded the bag down to close it and placed each bag on the floor. After he assembled each bag and approximately twenty bags, he placed them on the rear of the cart.

He then would drape a gray cape onto the rear of the cart. He stretched it over the rear of the cart and used some ropes to tie it down from the sides to the carts. Shlevko would then begin work in a project that would be very new and great. The project of Haploid Crystals. He would work on designing a vehicle that would drive and work off of haploid crystals. He would work on designing a vehicle that would drive and work off of Haploid crystals. He would work on designing a vehicle that would drive and work off of Haploid crystals. He also worked on designing batteries. The plans of the crystals would be to get very great performance and they would have a low decay rate on powering devices. The haploids would be carefully extracted from rocks by Shlevko and assembled together to design a variety of batteries and pcb panels with both a positive wire and a negative wire. Haploid crystals were like minature crystals and they would appear in an ore aggregate that would be mined from the earth surface. It would give customers; we have the right to refuse service from anyone; the opportunities to learn about and view videos and a sample of the aggregate.

The crystals are of a white fluffy looking a sparkling small near round size. He would mine these near his fall and winter home in the mountains. There would be great demand on these. They would be sold at the markets and customers would recommend the product to many customers and their friends. The Shlevko research team hoped that through research they found that the decay rate was so slow that the current voltage they provided would work almost four to thirty times longer then conventional technologies of alkaline batteries in electronics. It would be time for Shlevko to meet with the pilots from outerspace and he would phone them and they would answer their phone in the docking shuttle in the sky and told him they would come in to land now. Shlevko met them with a smile of excitement and a yeah of depress feelings of reservedness. I thought you guys would get here sooner, because my team wanted to show you a scientific assemblage of haploid crystals. His team were all family of brothers and more brothers. The pilots removed their helmets and set them in their cockpits and closed the craft doors to keep the animals, and insects from flying in. These are amazing as the pilots seen the work disk outside on the grass and could see the aggregate of the crystals and how the crystals sparkled into the room. Sergei makes most of his great work ready and he gets appointed the lead position and makes his own city in the forests. It is their he magically shrunk and lives in his miniature content.

The aero program would grow and soon their would be a salesman at a shopping mall and a guy would approach him slowly and introduce himself and he would tell him about Volcom and show him an orient bill showing Volcom as the skull, in black and a variety of orient symbols. Which would be of the language. He would walk on and the salesman would go to do something else. This building would be a large commercial building with glossy white floor in square tiles, and would have flourishing bright lights and there would be desk stands that the people that worked there would set on display the products that visitors would sell, and sales associates would tell the customers about and introduce them to them. There would be many dressed workers in silky pants and impressive shirts. There was a guy named Zac that lived in a large city and enjoyed aero technology and radio broadcasting. He would teach customers how to use a video cassette recorder to put content on video tapes for radio broadcasting and automatize the programming.

Thus the programs could be managed with the remote control and provide almost one hundred and four minutes of play on the air waves. Zac would meet Sergei in public in a store as he is shopping in a small building. The building would appear small of modern wood. The pilots were amazed and then see how it were arranged onto the pcb panels which had the circuits for a positive lead and a negative lead. They were impressed to observe that it would be powering cameras and electronic music devices. Shlevko told the guys that they could buy them at the market and here as well. He gave them a tour and showed them he put in garden places to grow grapes and the pilots walked slowly with him and liked the view. The grapes were of thick foilage and the grapes were wet to the looks and the ground around them as well. He would then show them where he would bottle juices for the markets and the markets and stores in the city as well as how he would bag the grapes for the stores. The pilots were impressed with how the changes have changed with their friend Shlevko. He told the workers that he was beginning to not have much success in board assembly with the haploid crystals because of voltage extraction and mentioned by probing them into the board that by chance they would deliver greater results then they already did. Shlevko what are your favorite colors? I have been quite happy with the colors we have been utilizing now on the air craft. Have you guys had any success on finding more people in space. Yes we have, we located a planet named Volcom and it has its own aerospace program and defense as well as its own freedom and a motivated market and great places to have fun. The Volcom planet a leader in nutruceutical and herbal remedies for the people on the planet and at Volcom. The aero space pilots would travel to a moon in space that would be kind of hot and the pilots would not attempt to step on the surface of the large planet. It would be possible to do so in the evening and it would turn out that this moon would be a great place to travel as the crafts would in stationary outerspace between the moon and a large shuttle and planet earth and other planets in space. Space would be dark the sky would be dark gray and the sun could be visible and many stories of shining stars. The atmosphere on the planet would be very thick and the planet would be a dusty dirty planet but would be livable with an exception to the daytime temperature and heat of weather. There would be some planets and not really noticeable amounts of ponds or lakes containing natural waters from the planet. It would be possible for the aerospace pilots to skim the surface as they traveled through and exit through the sky and travel across to another planet and determine whether it would be safe to land and or travel into the planet and fortunately the technology in the craft could obtain readings on the matters and toxicity of the planets before entering or landing on the planet. This would prevent the crafts from getting burnt or compressed in the atmosphere. The aerospace pilots would discuss the posibilities of placing an underground city on the planets which would make it more cool and habitual for planets that would seem of fiery heat and dryness during the day resembling a desert. Shlevko finished his day and earned quite a bit of money and commodities and he planned to increase his sales and purchase a house in the mountains. Shlevko would work to grow an additional several hundred feet of grapes and make them into gift and grocery bags and awesome and impressive great juices for many stores.

In the city there would be about nine markets and grocery stores approximately three. The city would be quite small and had not changed much. Later in the day some of the native people of the land would go to see Shlevko. They would bring supplies to demonstrate how to make jewelry. Hey Shlevko I'm Pooyan and this is Alverdio We would like to show you stones we use for jewelry and how we make good and incredible jewelry with Sterling Silver Wire and stones like amethyst and jade stones. As well as a combination of amethyst and sapphire. How clasps and barrel clasps would be crimped flat and smooth to the surface and individual bags were used for each bracelet and necklace. They would show how to make earrings and finger rings. He would be dazzled and amazed by the style and quality of the appearance of each of the stones, such as the definite smoothness and beautiful deep colors of the stones. There would not be any reason to have them shipped in as they were occurring normally through digging through the earths surface. Each of the stones found would require removing from the ore and then polishing to give it a jewelry appearance.

They then explained that presentation is important. We are using red, black, green, crushed velvet to place on display the jewelry and then we photo it and put them on sale on keep them on display for the customers. Shlevko would show the natives on assembling their first radio broadcasting station and how they could purchase broadcast extend which would network the stations further out around the city and the mountains. Shlevko was a respected and highly sought guy in the city and he would show the men how they would be putting together satellites for outerspace and he would go through the assembly proccess with them. The assembly is simple and not difficult you see there are two solar panel, two straight poles, the satellite body and the motivator motor. The solar panels help it contain charge and get voltage to the components and the motivator. During the time some people were sneaking through the yard and Shlevko scared them with a growl and claw of a bear. The men dirty in appearance ran back through the woods. Shlevko would begin to show them components and began by opening the rear of the cabinet as well. He placed aside the bolts in a container and used a fool to show the parts. The first board is the motivator board, the second is the logic board which does the broadcasting of audio, video and sends photography. The logic board also sends what time and has a compass mapping function to tell statistical data such as Fahrenheit and Celsius, altitude, water temperature, and work as a receiver of data and application of sending and receiving phone calls. It would also function as a security system and can take photos, record video, and audio and send the data to a ground based receiver. The third board is for signal displacement for defense and encryption of frequencies form ground based receivers. The fourth board beside it creates a signal path which creates a spread to add in frequencies for broadcasting. Thus made the Xanthium series and additional the ground based receiver could be sent and used anywhere on the planets and it has a folding antenna on the receiver that communicates to the satellite system and a proper keyboard for adjusting and working and using the capabilities of the satellite. The natives were amazed and curious about the prize but thought it would be easier to work with Shlevko for their project needs. Shlevko to the natives I would like to show you guys the older system is about half the size and the newer one has twice the memory. That is all for now, I do not have anything else to show you and explain to you today. I want to introduce you guys to my aero space friends. "Alverdio, Pooyan" Shlevko addresses the men this is the aerospace crew. Each of the men smiled at the natives in amazement "alright, yeah" the natives replied and men coughed with some humor as to how dumb founded they felt. The aerospace crew under the direction of Zac and Shlevko invited the natives to go with the aero space crew to see the planet Mulxee and the people agreed with the plans and security of satellites were increase on the property of Shlevko and literally non-stop photos and video security would take place from and through outerspace. Shlevko would get known as green cloud and recognition as a native to the additional natives. The aerospace men had everyone fasten their seat belts and latch down their head harness. Alright we are on our trip there. The aerocraft made some noise as electromagnetic systems powered motors and the crafts began to lift from the pads and climb the air and into space. The men showed each other it would be possible to play audio and music and as they began to exit to the starry sky they could see many Satellites around the planet and light from the moon. They made their path upward and flew to a shuttle base in space and then flew to and by the planet.

They entered the atmosphere and it would be thick and the surface hot and foggy like a terracotta desert and the craft would fly along the surface for many miles and then they would exit through the nights sky by flying out to the side of the planet. They then flew to the station in space and the crew there opened the door and invited them in. There would be dark green tiles, and small baskets with green plants in them. They had a couch and the guys could cook food in the room and exercise as well as shower and sleep. The room would have warm lighting and warm architecture. Some of the men made meals, others rested and some exercised.

Eventually almost all of them would rest and they would travel again the second day to the planet and then to the station where they would stay a few days. They would begin to travel back home and the aircraft drove to the atmosphere and entered the evening sky and landed on the pads slowly. They shutdown the craft and stretched. Alright lets get out and scrub and clean the crafts. The men removed their seat belts and lifted the air tight sealed door and climbed out onto the platform. Each of the natives and aero persons told each other to stretch, do some routine exercise. In which they would exercise for about fifteen minutes and each of the men would help carry hoses, and a bucket and rags, scrubbing brushes, pads and towels. They began by rinsing debri from the craft and filling the buckets on the platform with water and pouring in soap and adding more water to mix it from the hoses. The guys then cleaned that craft and three others on the platform. It took an hour and ten minutes and then about fifteen minutes to clean the inside of the aero crafts. It is this year that Zac comes out with an electronics brand and then work to build components that would produce advanced technologies for human use.

They would specialize in a project that would create technology in a more fascinating way with the development of haploid crystals, these gold sparkly crystals would produce impressive states because they would become a pcb style board that would clip inside many electronics of the future and the present. Zac would open a defensive training school and all the workers would be their including the instructor, he would name this school the Shorin Ryu Defensive. It would be popular around the country. It would include a cafe with coffees, fruit drinks, and donuts. This school flourished well for awhile and would close. It would be the year for the astro space program and what would be more thrilling would not be the crafts that would travel to space but would be Doctor Norrol's time travel work that would lead an inventor Chaz to help develop a device to record the imagery of the brain and during cognitive sleep to log where travel is taking place and recording the many events.

This would be used to thrill and to change the future and become more known. It would become a steady and dependable place for many events to be enjoyed. Jonnah would be a leader in the production of the renderance of this technology would be popular to the studios throughout the entire country and around the world. Jonnah would quote on how marketing would follow an algorithm of the keyword structure, name of the work, then this technology would be incorporated into firewire and marketed with ddt digital data transfer using qe quality element through rms routine marketing services. Jonnah would have his clients visit him and Jonnah would continue design promotions, strengthening and conditioning his business. Victor would discuss on audio and video coding and how as a stress alleviator to all his clients this would be some professional work by movie studios and would get recognition from other large scale commercial and industrial studios around the planet. Wendy would be in charge of packaging and Chaz would work in securities for the most lead part of Oleynik Studios, Welsh Wine Growers since 1999. Welsh Wine growers since 1999. Welsh Wine growers of Oleynik and welsh were like the swiss watch of wines and they Kene Welsh a Mathematician knew wines and economics of how the corporate process could do sales in excess of 760 billion dollars, and they would be the hazy capital wine industry with flavored punches that would set some people back. Kene Welsh the swiss watch Mathematician for the Oleynik Studios took much pride and happiness in the work of wine. Including with a prodigy Kyle a lead author and developer and scientist. "I'm a doctor and a scientist."replies Kyle. Kene Welsh the swiss watch mathematician for the Oleynik studios took much pride

14

and happiness in the work of Wine. Including with a prodigy developer and Scientist. I'm a doctor and a Scientist." Replies Kyle. Kene Welsh would be the developer of the swiss watch that would be used at wine growing places.

There would be a program titles Rebourg and those not familiar with this type of use would maybe or maybe not like any or all of the projects. There would also be the project of Roman candles. Rebourg would be about a guy that would get suited in plastic and wear a plastic body toy suit and would get the assembly of the bolts to make a figure. He would be in love with his counterpart.

The plastic conversion would be popular and almost as if the person had been getting their entire body coated or molded by wax to make the model or and a permanent suit. Shlevko would be ready to make his journey to America and he would rent some land and pay his brother who would lend the money to the landlord for his rent on the land. Shlevko would begin by tilling the land and cultivating the soil and then he would shower in back in a pond and then enter his brothers house to sleep. Shlevko began to sell dirt and to do so he would shovel an entire pile and with his brothers they would shovel and spread a tall pile and wet it down and setup a section for customers to bring their carts. Customers and merchants would come and load carts and buy dirt for their gardens and houses. Later he would prepare some coffee, eggs, and local papers for reading and would remove the garbage and put it in the trash to send. There would be a family in a city that would be secretly related to everyone in the world.

They would have to hide from the military because the military and Governments would take them in under arrest or kidnap them. This would be where routine driving military vehicles like humvees and jeeps would go to the peoples houses. It would turn out that these people would be Russian and be with money. This idea would be used from nearby restaurants as well as harry of the potter where a teacher takes off a whole year by chance. Sergei; as you will notice in this presentation when looking at this screen there are many satellites that go around the cosmic order. Each of the satellites will be taught in the program. I will discuss the Ergonix, one will notice they have three

15

short end antennas and these are used for about a few purposes. Ergonix is decided to use the system for basic communications which include dbm, wls, das, pud, vmud, and nls. Digital broadcast management, wireless link service, digital audio services, picture uplink downlink, video management uplink/ downlink and Navigation link system. This makes it no one of the most impressive satellite systems on the planet. It is used online by 460 thousand members.

When the communications company needs to move the positioning, they use a wlr wireless long range remote and this runs now electromagnetic engines and mapping sensors and photo sensors and temperature sensors to move it around in outerspace. Graciously the systems have the solar cells that collect the light like the photo and store it in rechargable cells that are used to power the device. I will now discuss on each of the features like dbm, wls, das, pud, vmud, and nls. Each feature for this system is modern and since none of the components are serviced or replaced during the lifespan of the systems in space. Digital broadcast management has been designed to manage the order and loads of audio to the antenna system for transmission uplink and downlink to the planets of the solar system. It is the actual part that communicates to stations on the ground. The wireless link service does the following; it manages the call and voice data for satellite phones.

The Digital audio service makes sure all audio for the wireless link service is relayed through integrated circuits as digitally counted audio. When companies need uplink and downlink programs for customers to their digital cameras and video players the picture uplink and downlink. It uses graphic interchange format to produce output files that are correlated to the content and then this content if any das is needed is routed to dbms for forward to the companies that make the equipment that will then receive the coded file and be programmed to display the graphic interchange format with das audio that happens to be programmed to play at the same frame rate of the video. When realtime frame rates are needed vmud may be used to do more online video management upload and downlink. It is more fast because no encoding is needed. Therefore each broadcast is almost live using das and wls to maintain overture and signal to each customer through each affiliated and subscribed customers. During the operation the satellites may encounter debri such as other space systems in space and the nls is composed to link using bls and gls which are brown link service and green link service which are both the frequency setup in arrays in an integer format and these arrays are computed to adjust the behaviors that make the craft work great and produce appropriate bls, gls, wls, dbms, and keep the systems connected. The system used to work with the feature is know as the Phalmat it is designed to be the master controller to the Satellite systems in space as well as to the network companies and subscribed customers. Commonly destricated as the PAK it comes on to customers and networks that have not determined how to communicate correctly to the Phalmat.

Because the programming has been designed to be sent in particular manners and communicated with as less errors as possible. The PAK lock displays on a black screen and in green font to ask the user for the Pak code to access the dbms through Phalmat. When the PAK code is right the systems connect and show the available subscribed programs. When the PAK is wrong the PAK will prompt again and because of the network, it may or may not connect to the network. What does happen is; when the user or technician fails to connect to the dbms the PAK may lock the screen and then after about 80 seconds it will become not grayed out and the PAK can be re-entered once again. This would be almost endless until the PAK is connected or blocked by dbms.

When the dbms accepts the PAK it may verify a new feature known as pud this uplinks a graphic image to the dbms and may contain a QR code which tells the dbms what to display, and handle all the services when dbms cannot read the pud it may retry again and uplink or download a replacement pud file. These are reliable because PAK has been designed to securely provide dbms and wls. When the PAK is blocked by dbms it can be fixed by verifying the PAK and having a technician load the pud files to the unit and ensuring that if it has small antennas that they are angled to receive signal and send signal and data to the company and subscribed systems. When a conventional dish is used for broadcasting and uplink/downlink you get a correct signal when the dish has been properly oriented to the network that it will be communicating with. The conventional dish has been getting replaced by the bnc antennas because they have been able to communicate with the Phalthom as well as meet the speeds of the Phalthom coding by as little interference of signals through its rubber coating insulator and its basic 18awg ground and now the european ground system. There has been many customers that have inquired on how the ground and now the european ground system. There has been many customers that have inquired on how the ground and european ground differ.

The european ground shows more grounding and displacement of interference. The factory ground is alright but only grounds electrical interference and most interference during its usage. The tech support for Phalthom is managed by the customer service team and the customers would call their companys to discuss any problems they have with their experiences using the equipment provided under contract or sold online by merchants throughout the entire world. When Welsh industries acquired many of the satellite companies they had upgraded much of the dbms's to allocate more wls through the satellite companies. They made pud more quicker with das audio and they help insure a more smoother wls to the networks and fixed the socket coding for pud and das to allow for wls to share the same communication bandwidth. Which what happened was the pud and das were able to encode almost all the data and dbms through pud and das and it would be very popular and the image quality would be literally photo paper quality in very high resolution and as clear as photographs to the viewers.

The das would be digitally recorded and would be as live as possible. This would describe the Ergonix satellite and the awesome features of this system. Now that we understand this technology more in detail, I will begin to lecture on another few satellites known as dln the satellites that use digital link network are designed to route the data sent through a dbms and wls and is maintained with gls. Each satellite by Ergonix would have the same terminology. Another company Telepacific is designed to manage phone calls and data to its customers. It does so by routing its phone calls and data to its customers. The satellites have an uplink and downlink service and the brains which are designed to get and route around the data to other places to send it to the network. Companies that relay the technology through programs to its customers. The PAK is a common gate keeper for the Telepacific Satellites Company. Almost all of the satellites are engineered to compose through transmission digital audio of some kind normally put together in digital audio which means that it can be played, paused, rewinded, fast forward and it can also be mastered by companies to other satellites or control boxes, because of the digital time scale property that is used to track the dlns (Digital Link Network Service). At a given time the PAK is unique for each satellite and the hex key is used to access that network whether public, military, Government or otherwise setup. Each satellite communications with a controller and the controllers use each hex key as an account for the customers and the hex key is truly provisioned to connect to the programs and services on the account. When customers do not pay their bills to the merchants, the hex key may be deleted or the programs and services may be discontinued to the customers and may be restored when the bills get paid and law enforcement agencies may over see this and the activities that take place on customers accounts.

Criminal activity and fraud is not permitted on most networks and the accounts are usually suspended or demoted because of the activities and in the most cases legal defenses are taken and proper law and military and Government sectors are contacted to ensure the safety security and privacy of its members in accordance to the law.

PATS also known as public access terminal systems are commonly easy ready access connections that allow users to connect to the networks for mobile communications such as radio for scouts and mapping systems. AMPS Airport Mobile Portable Systems is designed to provide at live broadcast flight information; guides, maps and service locations. NCGS Navigation Compass Guide Service is designed to give das directions to customers on where to drive and guide with the accuracy of compasses to map systems. MAVL music audio video layer is a format that makes photo paper quality video broadcasts and encodes the audio layer with the imagery in a form of MAVL composing Graphic Interchange Format and audio layer. EALS European audio link service helps customers communicate with their vehicles by being able to unlock or lock or remote the trunk doors and alarm. WASL Woodland Active Link System is designed to link product information to satellites and entertainment companies and manufactures of audio products. VAS Visual Aid System designed to assist handicapped customers with the content in more enhanced methods. DAYTS Do As Your Told System is designed for military and Government businesses to track supplies, inventory, and notes recorded. TDS Team Development System is designed to permit uplink/downlink of data for projects and upgrades. FBS Free Booter System; The free booter system is a description of networks that do not hall any security and customers can connect to them. An open accessible public device. Currently many of the satellite systems are using the freebooter system however this has been commonly used with conjunction of an encoded card that would connect its presence. When the satellite systems need repair is is commonly done by changing bak1 to bak2 and wls to wlsbak2 and this changes the settings to almost a duplicate of the parts. After this the systems are retired or upgraded or the data from the dbms is copied to the planet and the service is ended by letting the satellite fall down to the earths atmosphere trash level. In this situation the satellite disposes of itself in the trash. The next topic we will discuss how to load the pud and how to put files on the pud.

The encoded cards or pud card is loaded by universal serial bus. The folders to be created are pud, wls, cache and upldnl. The pud folder will hold the image used to connect to the network or satellite companies. The wls folder will save and keep data for connectivity and location on satellite network. The cache will store data and junk data that is cleared routinely without affecting performance. The cache is cleared during the day. The upldnl; uplink downlink folder contains files and stuff requested by the users. It is a private folder on the encoded card. There may be an additional folder PAK; to store the access code and accounts which contain the hex codes for each account. To be managed by the dbms of the satellite networks. The encoded keys may be preloaded and activated online and may also be rented by dealers around the world. When the accounts are lost or stolen the hex key can be canceled with the satellite networks and through the dealers. Many Satellite companies will have their own liscense agreement, privacy policy, and limited warranty program and these will discuss some very important information. Limited Warranty; The technicians at Tele Pacific Satellites have worked and researched hard to assemble quality and great electronics and have put together this limited warranty and manual to assist the customers. If for some reason further technical support is needed, please call your local dealer, technician and factory for repair of the unit or part needing repair.

Tele Pacific Satellites has included a limited warranty that is valid for 80 days. During this timeTele Pacific Satellites will repair or authorise repairs or replacement of parts and software for the units. After the 80 days limited warranty it will be at the discretion of the technicians, dealers, and authorised repair persons to make adjustments, modifications, or repairs to the units. The limited warranty excludes misuse, neglect or damage from improper use or failure to properly install the units. It may not cover commercial exhibition without permission from the factory, dealer or authorised repair persons and technicians. The warranty begins upon delivery and extends to cover claims and to fulfill the repair or replacement of the units. To locate a technician or repair center contact Telepacific.com/guide/roats repair or authorised technician service guide. Privacy Policy, many companies have a privacy policy that discloses how information is used, obtained or collected from users and if and how it is shared to third party companies for marketing and information purposes.

Privacy Policy: For the convenience of the customers this site has decided to use this privacy policy. What we do with your information; when customers visit our site we may log details that help further improve the technology, products, and services that we offer. We may also request information such as the name, email address, and the customers age range. We may implement cookies to collect data and to help track performance and help with storing data for future usage. The customer may remove the cookies and request that the data is not stored. We will never rent, sell, lease or trade the customers information without the consent of our customers. The customer information may be disclosed to third party advertisers upon request.

California Online Privacy Policy Act; The customers must be 18 or older to visit the website and to make purchases or subscribe to services including interaction with third party services. An exception, customers under the age of 18 or not adult may browse the site with a parent or guardian. Any and all interactions on the site is responsibility of the customers and it is the responsibility of customers and it is the responsibility of the customer to abide by the policies, agreements, privacy policy and any license agreements. Customers may also need to review any third party sites, and sites not ran by this site. Should the customers have any questions about the privacy policy they can contact us below for assistance. This policy is updated and modified from time to time and the date of this is shown on the privacy policy. This policy was last updated on July 8, 2017. By using this site the customer agrees to hold harmless Tele Pacific for all claims, damages, and liabilities that may arise and that there are no warranties implied or expressed in the contents, technologies, software, and products therein.

This will include both seen and unforseen claims in applicable law, including from misuse, nature, and usage of the data and products. In respect to customer privacy accounts may be deleted, closed or suspended when not being logged into for periods of time. Accounts may also be banned or blocked from services and purchases for failure to comply or follow the agreements on this site and other sites that have decided to use this policy.

TelePacific Return Policy on Merchandise, Items may be exchanged or replaced with another item at the same price of purchase. The proof of sales slip may be needed. The customer may have to prepay the postage or get postage return approval. If the sales slip cannot be located the item may be exchanged at the discretion of the management team. Customers may return and exchange items for a period of 80 days. Liscense Agreement of Tele Pacific Communications. This agreement is between the customers, subscribers, and advertisers, and Tele Pacific communications. Tele Pacific works and researches is products and services to be as put together as correctly as possible by the technical manuals and manufacturing processes. Billing for payments is to be made to the dealer, company, authorized representative to be paid to the accounts.

The billing cycles begin on the 14th of each month and payments posted or not paid by the 14 day is considered late. The not paid payments and payments made after the 14th are subject to late penalties. The late fee is $19.00 for each account. Termination of Service, When an account is not paid the service may be terminated as accounts remain unpaid during the months and canceled by the following due date.

Warranty of Service, the customers, users, and subscribers agree to hold harmless for any and all liabilities and damages that may result during the usage of the services, programs, and billing processes, billing payment plan and unpaid account balances. This includes from misuse, incorrect setup, mishandling, neglect, failure to properly service, handle and use all equipment. Telecommunications offered by TelePacific may require that an agreement of a one year or two year contract be made to make payments on equipment. Equipment payments are made on the 14th and late there after and unpaid after the following 14th. Equipment may be returned and accounts may be requested to be canceled. When the total balance is paid on equipment, the customer may keep the equipment. They may need a new contract for new equipment. Telepacific may cancel the liscense agreement for any reason with or without notice but may provide notices to its customers. For example if the equipment is not in compatible network range, the agreement may be canceled and the contract may be canceled. The customer may be referred to a compatible provider and a technician may be scheduled to setup the equipment for the customers, subscribers and the advertisers. TelePacific claims on service and equipment may be resolved with the dealers, merchants, subscribers, dealers and technicians.

TelePacific claims on service and equipment may be resolved with the dealers, merchants, subscribers, dealers and technicians. The problems will be resolved in timely manner and any disputes will be handled in accordance of the law. TelePacific may be contacted by calling emailing or visiting their website at www.telepacificcommunications.com. This concludes our class schedule for this week on these topics. Please clean your desk area and dispose of any trash to the waste basket on the way out. There will be a quiz on course work tommorrow. Sergei decides to work in cleaning computers for his friends. He does so by setting up the work desk and carefully setting the central processing unit on the desk. The horizontal units that lay flat being the desktop unit and the units that stand vertical are the tower units. The servicing on each machine differs by the manufacturing model and servicing schedule by technicians. Sergei would need to make sure that he understands safety information when working with electrical equipment. Most all pcs are serviced by making sure the unit is not powered on or plugged in to its power supply.

When working with components, durable vinyl or latex gloves are used to handle components and parts such as memory, solid disk drives, pc cards, and circuit components that require handling them. This exception would be fans, power supplies, and disc and disk drives. Sergei would need to unbolt or unscrew the coves on the frame to repair, replace, clean or modify components. He would use cleaner, a damp cotton towel and wipe the dirt and dust from inside and then dry with another cotton towel. Then the covers would be re-aligned to the slots and then snap them back securely into place. After the machine dries inside the computer may be plugged into its power supply and powered on or tested to see if it powers on, loads and restarts or shutsdown. Sergei decides to go for pet supplies for his pets and to give them a ride through the scenic country to go have pie with his friend that works on sales of pet supplies. He would go to see his friend and they would work on his sports car and change his rims for him.

Tbey would drive back and visit seawalk and see great amazing things from the ocean and exit seafood and specialty sandwiches. His friend and him would stay at their camper and they would go for a scenic drive and to some bars with some of their other friends and party for the week and take turns sleeping and partying and then drive all the way back to his office. The Niplais company begins to really research on how electromagnetic technologies can be further built to result in the vehicles during further then ever. They work on manufacturing components, electronics, and the interior, dash, rear bench, and necessary interior and trunk components. The final products produced are ready for the technicians to test, add the manuals, and enter it into inventory. Sergei would get a letter in the mail addressed to his address for the job position of a music performer for a show called Radio Wang Country. The show Wang Country would be really popular to Americans around the country and around the planet. Wang Country would be hosted by authentic real age Westerns that would travel and know a lot about the west and how the west had an affect on the culture.

The midwest was known for lots of archaeology discoveries in the west and numerous publications to news media outlets. Welcome everyone to Wang Country this show presents on topics of boating, fishing, archaelogical finds, old salons, dining and hosting. During the last eight weeks we had the opportunity to interview barbers, auto mechanics, dining restaurants, and people from the old west, we also topic on the mining industry. TelePacific would be one of the first Satellite companies to host this show and Ergonix would also host it in pud format with das. The company Oleksunik would become one of the leading manufacture for equipment for Telepacific. I would like to begin by discussing about the archaeology that has taken place over the last few years."Most Certainly," replies the guest." Most of the work is done in the removing of massive amounts of rocks and soil and digging into the surface of the earth in an effort to find fossils, and remains and items of importance. The finds are put in a bucket called finds and they are put on display to other scientists and publications are made to show the finds to readers around the world. It is often that the items get put on a showcase. The items can be marketed by campaigns. One of my favorite activities to do is gardening and for the people that do not have much experience they will see when doing it that it is not that difficult.

The important put about gardening is that the customer uses great planters, reads the labels, knows what their planting, and when soil is a must or dirt, that adequate soil is usable for the duration of the flowers. The gardener would begin by making sure that there is no weeds and grass and deep roots that would need to be removed by pulling them and discarding them from the dirt and fresh soil. The customer would safely remove each bunch of flowers from its sale container and after digging a hole deep enough to plant them. The flowers would be put in the hole and the soil would be spread back into place to present all the flowers.

The database management systems designed by llixotronics would be a cluster based server and there companies would do business all around the globe. The database would be designed to work using socket based processor boards to utilize memory and hard disk capacity and video graphics. The problem with llixotronics 272ARM, 272ARM-G, 272ARM-M processor would be that the program would lag and require a smaller user interface which would inquire about eighty percent less system resources and produce and consume sixty percent less energy then previous revisions of the program. Thus the ARM processor would be developed and it worked by clustering memory and processes to pass it and mobilize it to a network. The digital bnc antenna using a minature linear amplifier to electronically boost the signal in either input and output. The digital display has made it possible to look at the highs and lows of compression and expansion of all signals. The linear amp has been designed to expand or compress the output signal and what the customer gets is a more greater communications experience. The linear amp how signals have been experienced across many social networks and through telecommunications.

How to deal with video graphic errors and resolution issues has been difficult but typically most technicians will begin by updating the driver or finding the proper graphic driver for the video adapter. When it is constantly on error it is replaced by uninstall and adjusting the video display settings. Video graphic acceleration has been designed to handle all the loads of data that a computer can process and handle for any duration of tasks. The video graphic adapter cannot buffer most of the digital audio and therefore requires an onboard audio cart like a pc compliant adapter and the audio would buffer can be soft but it normally goes about 30, 60, 90, 100% in about a few seconds and has a bit rate of about 60, 84, 178 Kbps, and rare occasions of 500, 700, 900 Kbps. Many users experience that the audio cannot be heard in the speaker systems, audio systems or audio devices.

26

Pheobee would become the second maker of Satellite systems for home and supply office use. Pheobee an athletic guy, 37 years old, dark black hair, blue eyes, went to school and graduated to develop an electronic Satellite System called the Phe sat which would employ a group of people to make the Jaca OS. The Phe would include a graphical user interface and would come with technologies such as pan and spotter technology which would allow the owner or leasee of the system to adjust the way the signal would soak around the city mountains and wooded areas by coating against the surface and using the spotter to broadcast a series of video and mapping systems. They would include sensors for precision to the second temperature in Fahrenheit and Celsius. It would also have sensors for altitude, airspeed, and distance.

The system would include pressure sensors, motion and tilt sensors. Lets describe Pheobe os, it would be considered small and yet for all of its customers it would do telephone, audio and video sharing, webmail, weather and mapping. For those that have not visited a mall, there would be a mall and it would be a one floor mall and there would be an suburban vehicle crashed into the fountain and where the water would be like a fountain pool to the steps. There would be no one in the vehicle as it lies in the fountain. Phoebe would become a third largest Satellite business for many lands. Phoebe ETS would provide extended telemetary systems for other life places in space. This would typically work for the moon. The moon would be a mysterious place and from the surface it would look like not much more then a place with sand and much dirt that would encompass the surface. It would be from this planet that the people would ride a shuttle that would travel up to the moon and when it would land we would meet a civilization in the moon.

To the visitors surprises there would be long hard plastic constructed water slides that would travel from the craters of the moon all the way down to the center of the moon. It would be there that we would travel around and to do so we would ride in a taxi that would appear blue and along the tunnels and the bridges it would literally camo and disappear as the bridges and tunnels would be lighted blue and would intermix with the cars. It would be one of the first cities that have constructed many water slides and tunnels as freeways and roads that vehicles and non-heavy trucks could drive to the slides and their wheels and the vehicles could cruise along and drive along the slide to the places and roads, trees, and people were wanting to meet. It would be the season that Vivian would star in many episodes of Second Hospital and she would appear in various roles; she would be the patient in most roles and a house keeper and a desk worker in other roles. She would also be a singer and performer of hiphap music oldies music and exotic western moments.

She would sing the album Phoebe in the Winter and would record several albums. Many people would really enjoy Vivian as a star in SH Second Hospital she would build her fame and be the manager and owner of large apartment complexes. Vivian would work on electronics during the week.

She worked a hard work schedule and would be promoted to assistant manager at the stores that specialize in merchandise like component and element put togethers. As we drove in the moon we decided to stop and introduce ourselfs to some of the people there and we would learn from their culture that they were indigenous people and that they had maybe been to planet earth before and traveled through space to explore. The indian groups would know how to sew and make clothing, sports wear, jackets, pants, and would know about wood working, building bridges, buildings and space technology, sales and shopping.

We would travel and would eventually travel on a gravel dirt road to a house to meet some people that lived on the moon. We would meet the ruling supremacy government the king and queens for the planet city and would observe on our way there a sword stuck in the ground beside the dirt road. We would meet the prince of moon and his brothers and sisters. The cities through the moondom would be really clean and much care would be taken to keep the trash and recycles off the grounds, buildings, alleys, roads and the water slide tunnels. This would include the roofs, bushes, trees, mail boxes, and many crazy places to find trash. The prince would dress in all black but normally they would be dressed in many colors of clothing. The prince would be really into ball play and he would be noteworthy for almost an entire section on how he would work with shadows and sundials to be powerful in mapping and technology through the moon. It would be a black supremacy for many sectors of the moon and though the indians would have the skin color of being tanned and dark caucasion they would be very busy writing about the history and the gardening of the moon and how they arrived and put together the amazing places that would be below the sun drawn and inset.

The moon cities would be an impressive place to visit through few people would see it because when travelers would come to visit the green aurora would spin and shield out the exterior of the cities from asteroids, rocks and things from deep places in space. The nuggets on the planet were ore of the things that would ocassionally arrive from space and they would break down upon the surface and crack, break, and become debri. The cities would have a central Government, and parks, woods, mountains, rivers, and wildlife, and insects all around. We would travel back from the moon to planet earth and would share our stories and events with our friends and our companies that would be stake holders in our businesses. For the likeness of green goo, cake sloppy, mud slide and orange sliming people that constantly interacted on apparatus shows through the earth. It would be the idea to share these things with the alien civilizations on the moon and get them to sponsor and setup these events in the cities on the moons.

There are many moments in ponder of great events and a plastic coated toy is an impressive outcome in these civilizations. Phoebe Satellite Systems would create Phoe2700, Phoe2732, Phoe2752, Phoe2762, Phoe2772, Phoe2800, Phoe2900, Phoe2950 After about thirty years they would become a sub carrier and become Niplais 1700, and Niplais 1900. It would be in that same year that the satellite would drift off its orbit and fall into the trash and be crushed into a gazillion pieces. The Niplais space program would launch a few and put more Satellite systems into space. They would have a newer communication structure called Nep, Nepos, Neptel, Nepuds, NepMPS, Nepmgs, Nepvas and Nepllctrlrs. They would benchmark heavy N-audio and extremely fast video buffer technologies. The

Nepos would be an integrated computered component that would run on nes and integrated programming. The Neptel would manage the customers calling hardware. The Nepuds uplink, downlink, service would be for communications. Nepmps for maps, Nepmgs for vehicles to communicate and gather maps. Nepvas for video and audio systems to manage the audio and video programming and where the data would go. Nepllctrlrs would be for latitude and longitude controller systems for the orbit and positioning on satellites. Neptws would become a system that would route tires and wheels shops to its customers.

The Niplais company would open tire shops in stores and would sell six designs of tires and six designs of wheels and two sporting wheels and two sporting tires to make a display of a new tires product made from a spider web compound that would makeup the rubber of the tread on the tires. The plan of these tires as with the implementation of this compound to make the components of the vehicles; is that; the compound would reduce friction; heat from friction, tolerate more heat, have impressive performance, acceptable performance and be very quick and fast on a racing performance track. When automobiles would need to deal in more heat, work in more difficult environments or deserts driven by military trucks.

The spiderweb compound would be engineered to make the parts that would make up the frame monitor, drive system, and almost every component including the body, the hood, the top, the trunk, the dash, and any motors, components that would need to be cooler longer, run faster and be more driven to meet and exceed satisfaction. This technology would makeup almost all the vehicles and electronics, computers and parts made by Niplais and Volcom robots. They would research in making speakers, heat sinks and fans. There would be entire notebook personal computers built and crafted and the molds would be fabricated out of the spidergoop to make the chasis and the components and the hard disk, memory, processor, and video graphic components and assemblies would all be done and completed on spider built technologies. Very Cost effective and highly capable of making a pleasant spider enriched experience. Most of this material has been published before. The Electromagnetic Induction Photo

Sensor radio would become the most difficult technological feature for the moon planet and the Space Radio Programs. The object would be for the photo sensor to collect light and the electromagnetic induction coil would utilize a visual and audio trimmer to hear the frequencies in space and around the planet. When the colony was built on the moon, the city decided to also build the underground city that would be below the earth.

This would include vast roads that would indure secretly. There would be very long underground expressways that would stretch for miles and miles and cars would drive through underground caverns and the drivers would see all sorts of calcites & stalcites to the side of the road and over head the roadway. The road would be of damp silica and would be a little wet to the drive. The Niplaus cars would incorporate for the first time in the automotive manuals a positron transmode and positron shift. The positron would be a technology that would make almost seamless and accurate shiftings between all the gears. The positron tech would make vehicles impressively quick and dependable. Many of the vehicles architecture would be of spiderweb compound build and would be all electric by electromagnetic means. Positron thus became the fast and dependable seamless shift alternative. There would be a new phone service called Jaison and it would be designed to provide digital radio, music, maping directions, and good data for its customers. Designed by Sergei in the mountainous region in the west during the years 1970 to 1993 and then he would work with some of his friends that were metaphysical engineers to create the Jaison5555 and it would use a high tech controller to map the distance and steering with the maps and also allow for stationary test drive in neutral to practice driving the accelerator and braking and the driving skills on virtual maps to drive any destination and figure out which is the best arrival at the destination. There would be many technicians. For almost all the data maps around the world.

They would use many communication companies that would work on the maps that would be aggregated to the vehicles through dbms, and lat long map systems. There would be the option to plug up modems for Tele Pacific Communications and network data providers in the vehicles. The manufactory would simplify the components and the vehicles would consist of the mechanical, electrical and the electronic component systems. The vehicles would include a few safety features, such as electronic mechanical brakes, safety belts and anterior air bag system. The airbag system would deply only in the event of compression to the front of the frame side walls or rear posterior which would cause the pressed switches to inflate the safety airbags. The Niplaus company would develop a digital voice prompt computer that could surf the internet and read the website pages outloud to the readers and they could also play games, listen to music and see small images of the photos on a 3" screen to view about the discussions. The concept of Niplaus is to provide and manufacture the most impressive and robust dedicates of electronics for sale to the markets.

It began with the samples of deodorizer for vehicles and consisted of a blue lemon cleaner that could remove smells from vehicles. The second by product that would be recommended would be a glass of vinegar and it would be used to refresh a room and eliminate the smells that were present from tobacco, musk, body odor, pets, hauling of products and outdoors equipment. It would come in a small labeled bottle and include the instructions. The company CO2V would be a soda company. It came to be in 2011. The products would be ultra blends of fruit punches, natural grape and orange to make impressive drinks for anyone that likes to buy and consume sodas. The output quality mostly samples and yet amazing marketing tool.

The company CO2V is an American company founded by the Niplaus Company and its laboratories. The Niplaus laboratories designed in 2003 was focused on radio broadcasting, odor removal products for home, office and business use. The Niplaus labs designed nutrition programs to enhance mental clarity, body and aero space perceptions. The Niplaus Company designed aero crafts, underground cities, vehicles, boats, SM band radio, electromagnetic vehicles, broadcasters, data retrieval and built large viewing theater display units. Many are conceptual units are goals that are worked on by many technicians that assist these companies. The Digital Data Recovery Action has been designed to discuss how data is managed, the privacy and about transparency and how it is shared and when for advertising purposes. DDRA has the goal to manage data given by customers and provide customers the options to opt out and cancel their membership. The DDRA compliances are that the agreement require that the users be 18 or older and the certificates on the websites can view or see the settings of DDRA on a computer. The website can then optionally collect this data inputed by the customers through the wizard and manage it on their pc and this is possible to update on all websites that participate in the DDRA.

The customer data provided is important. These policies make how the data is managed between sites and third party sites through the entire internet. Along time ago; as many people may have had a similar experience, there was me and Jim and he would give me a ride as with a few others to a doctors. I would explain to him what if there was this family that was related to everyone in the outside world. There would be a few days that people would see military vehicles like jeeps and humvees. The orange balisor electric line weights were the age and definitely set the scene. With the idea that the military and the Government and people from around the world would seek out and take back with them people related to everybody. The magic in this would be a family related to everyone in the world but secretly in that this knowledge would not be shared with everyone. The electrical energy of the human body and nature of the balisor balls make this an amazing and impressive story of fiction.

Driving on the mountainous roads I would slow my vehicle which happened to be a car beside another car and the driver in the other car would shoot me with a needle extractor syringe and I would remove it and close my windows and drive as I would try to remove by squeezing my leg a white pus as it would would need to be removed. I would drive further around the bend and we would be driving into an entrance stall and there would be one after another of entrance stalls that would bend in as the vehicle would drive through each one and hopefully none of them would lock until the car would reach the end ; otherwise the vehicles would get stuck in a few stalls or break a stall or crash by getting stuck in the stalls. The other vehicle would chase to the side of the vehicle and there would be many cars driving through the stalls and to the outlet of the road to the other side. The cars to the front of me and to the sides and my car would make it in that traffic path to the other side and we would continue to drive. I would not see the other vehicle but presume they thought I needed their help medically but I did not. That would be a surprise for me. The vehicles people and I would notice during this time were gasoline fueled 6 cylinder or 8 cylinder motors. When it would come to development of a car in the past, I would design car motors of an 12 cylinder motor to a 14 cylinder motor. The spider web compound would make up the build of the engines and the architecture of the vehicles. The build would commonly be square or an x-block design. The home or office big screen theater system would be the design of great deal. Many people online had designed some of the most fascinating theater systems. The screen quality of 50 to 60 inches diameter. It would work on the wall, it could place it on the ceilings as well. It would be built using two to three sliding cases that would cover the front of a crt color 15" or 17" digital apparatus or lcd display. The first box would go around the screen to tunnel the picture and this box would be sealed to keep the light inside. The second box would have about a 3" diameter and on the side it would use a photo page magnification sheet and this would be firmly attached inside. From the outside three hinges would be installed for a mirror that would be used to angle the display to the wall ceiling or viewing section.

The focal would be adjusted in the box with the oval lense and a small handle would be used to do the measurements of the focal quality for the picture. Typically when making these settings, they do not have to be modified or changed that often because the focus is constant for the displays. The final touch for Niplaus Theater Systems is the wood casing construction and the build would be crafted by several people and use machine screws to build the final product and any paints or lacquers would be applied then and the sales price, user manual, and booklet would be placed together with a universal programmable remote, optional speakers, cables and packaging to be placed in a box. The boxing tape and packaging crews would then tape the boxes closed and affix the labels for marketing and advertising purposes. To experience the most excellent picture quality, it has to be as clear as possible. To achieve this, the viewing room needs to be as dark as possible. The remote should use fresh batteries and should never mix used because it can damage electronics. To prevent interface problems make sure the remote is plugged with the battery compartment lid and no, the remote should be angled at the sensor to get a great signal. To enjoy the maximum reception the customers will want to use one remote at a time to prevent interference or over code which jams the signal or prevents a proper response from happening. Some functions may not work on a remote because not every device has all the features or the customer may need a different code that can be found on the web and it may be used to enable additional features on the remote for the devices available. Many electronics when plugged in to an outlet have a problem with electric him in the electric box lines, this can lead to whine and the sound quality of the speakers to contain a hum in the operation of the audio. This problem is corrected when the user checks the ground plug and makes sure is is snug and may use a surge suppressor and a line filter to plug a supply strip into, to reduce all the humming sounds caused by ground and electrical interference.

Through the electric line. The line filters role is to filter all the interference by electronically correcting the noise in the electric line. Understanding Surge Suppression and how to deal with the ground plug. The Niplaus company has designed a AC Grounding System using Aerotech technology. It works by using alligator clips to a pcb to an external outside ground wire and grounding stake. The alligator clip goes on the third prong ground and makes electronic grounding to the outdoors. Indoors and outdoors the cord system and the receiver make grounding a more pleasant and dependable experience and help filter line noise in the electric lines. Prouding a dependable output source and great weather and voltage suppressor. The Oleynik company would engineer some amazing things. The first would be license agreements, privacy policies and terms and conditions papers and warranty agreements. My company would develop the new method of cladding together carats of amethysts and making a gold glitter leafing foil to clad it to actual terracotta and gray rocks that would be worker crafted and oven built and produce amethyst gold rocks, bullion, and jewelry pendants. The Oleynik business would produce reading literature and years of entertainment to its customers and fans. The outcome would be professional grade marketing and it would get 5 star ratings in the appearance on how the material would be unique, very creative and educational to all walks of life. MDI and TDS technologies would produce an Satellite Component that would become high demand. It would make data saving to 16k and it would expand to 40GB to store military slot schedule data with information data. It began with 16k data which would store about 80 pages of gui keyboarded text. When it expanded to 40 GB it became almost unlimited pages of storage. The uplink and downlink were a slow ethernet component over an infrastructure of an internet protocol using webless and users would access through the internet and the input would be file to open and save, and a print option for a dot matrix printer. The memory would use a w9 controller and could save internally to its computer. MDI and TDS became a very fast information exchange company. Brubeard became a compliance standard for the computer which would do no more then to save text files to its memory. Synatron Karoke machine Satellite became the first Karoke machine in outerspace by Oleynik business. The machine provided on the clock recording and it would be done through the internet on a computer and the Karoke machine would have all the electronic controls in software and they would adjust the music that would be performed one person at a time through Synatron's Digital Management Engine. Durell Homeographic Satellite System became a leader in the carbon spread print tracking of termperature fluctuations and carbon in the businesses and homes to provide accurate technology.

It helped customers manage, fans, doors, vehicle locks, cleaning robots, data, personal work desk using technology similar to MDI and TDI with Synatron Karoke but at expensive but affordable recording packages. Viszee medical therapeutic remedies became the largest producer of oral supplements to treat the spread and growth of cancer in patients being treated by their doctors. Viszee would provide guide counseling for the treatment of cancers. Durell Homeographic would make available networks of doctors, pharmacists, and packages of health plans, coverages, and client review through an MDI-TDI similar system to include a low graphic gui which would let its customers see the person they are chatting with, and enjoy all the services and products through Durell in a home, office, medical center. The Durell Homeographic Systems typically consist of a gui which includes a set top box, keyboard, and internet connection. The customers and users would need their login information for Durell to connect. It is typically provided by doctors, and providers to their patients and is billed to their insurance providers, medical offices and approved billing addresses. The Durell Homeographic System can connect to a printer and the doctors can print to the printer and prescription and drug information can be completed at a network of pharmacies through referral of Durrel Homeographics, and Durrel Homeographic Medical Care. Katel Synacone Satellites began the all to rage when they developed a new photo collecting pan cell and began to put the first restaurant in space that would cook, corn dogs, chicken, potatoes, pizza and hot menu foods and cold drinks served all day in brown paper bags and delivered to customers from all around space and on the moon.

The ovens would be made from pizza boxes which would be sized to have a viewing window in the top, baking sheet aluminum foil, and magnification sheet for the cooking heat. The Solar sun begins by heating through the viewing window to heat the foil and heat it enough to build food dishes on it. The restaurant called Gourmet Space Foods would ship its food to its 82 restaurants along the cities. The restaurants would inquire on the menu and the bags were shipped by crafts from outerspace in an hour. Introducing the new led display data management processing entertainment computer. It features one amp, double array audio, signal perception speakers. The light emiting diode display would have etched print screen inside dark screen. It would include operating instructions that would teach various methods to enjoy the entertainment and web companion with a small 5.5" screen to view to the pictures on the web. Web companion would be an I/O input output interactive talking and conversation browser. The computer would be popular for simple role playing gaming and interaction to more then many users using the led resolution which would transform to a rectangle matrix display of led lamps that could multi colorly perform the builds of shapes, patterns, and user content. It would have its own webmail and music and digital content. It would have connections for small versatille keyboard, microphone, earphones, and network connections. Beginning with the assembly of each machine I would look and determine what type of computer I have and then begin by looking at the connectors behind the computer and look at the plugs of the items that will be plugged in. The items like keyboards, mouses and keyboards are referred to as I/O Input Output Devices. The Display comes in varieties of models like CRT Cathode ray tube, led light emitting diode, and lcd crystalline display using backlighting. The common plugs are the standard Vga known by video graphic adapter. The other plug known as video patch and HDMI. These are known as the graphic user interface. They are powered by a 3 prong and 3 slotted plug that connected properly power the display to a 115 VAC power. The next device is the keyboard and mouse, each are either AT, PS/2 and USB Universal Serial bus respectively.

The AT Cable is very old circa 1990s and the PS/2 is more modern but is being replaced by the USB plug. The USB powered plug and the PS/2 and AT plug are both powered by the computers power supply to the computer. The internet is typically connected several ways: The first is wirelessly the second is by ethernet and the third is by telephone and the fourth is by dock. This is considered an input output device. The pc slot is used to slot, cards to make phone calls, fax definer, video for a gui through vga and to plug audio cards and recording cards in to mix and I/O audio. When graphic systems are bad on the computer they are changed or repaired by installing a vga video graphic adapter pc slot card. These are typically different sizes depending on the model of the computer and the brand. These are installed using rubber gloves and draining excess energy from the power supply.

To do this: The machine must be disconnected from the power cable by removing the power plug from the wall or power supply terminal and pressing the power button in and holding it for several seconds to drain power from the circuits. I would like to note that this does not drain from the battery on the processor for the clock. The battery is designed to be usually a button cell size battery and it is needed to keep the time and date and store various settings for the central processing unit. When the date and time are constantly wrong

38

on the machine; the battery may need to be replaced. This is done by making sure the computer is unplugged and removing the excess energy to ground. It to the technician work base. If voltage is not removed the cpu may be hazardous to touch. When the battery is replaced the technician will need to power the computer and when the bios appears, the computer may have changed to the factory settings and depending on the scenario of the computer; only the time and date may need to be updated and saved to the cpu.

Further settings that may need adjusting are the boot sequence; and operating system load mode. For many computers they typically consist of order of hard disk, removable media and digital reading drives. If the customer needs to load the operating system, they will need to enable and turn off the installation mode. When using the computer, customers may find that particular applications, games and videos require more work desk memory then others. This is contingent on the amount of memory also this memory is the random access memory. This works by storing memory and being skilled enough to access each of the applications and pages being worked on. If the memory seems to slow, it may be upgraded or changed if it seems hot and slow. Thus depending on the brand and model more memory may be added to improve performance and speed of the computer. When the computer is performing slow the memory may optimized through programs.

The brains of the computer is known as the Winchester Disk and it is composed of data writing and reading at a particular speed for example 5400 RPM and is installed in capabilities of 40,60,80, and 100 GB. It has two plugs IDE Interface plug and Sata the two depend on the brand model. There are many computers that have adapters for the IDE and Sata typically does not use an adapter. Depending on the type of software the customer will need to setup partitions of the operating programs, file storage, and temporary cache. The files are first copied and then the setup resumes and installs additional files and applications. When the hard disk is low on storage space, an additional disk drive can be added on many computers. Many customers decide to store their files in cloud storage and removable media. If the hard disk fails, it may be serviced by technicians to move the data disks from the spindles to a replacement drive.

When the drive responds properly the computer should work with the gui to produce the content loaded to the computer when the cpu has video errors, audio errors and data errors and constantly freezed it may need the cpu board changed. Typically these come with the processor but may be updated with the one from the older machine to fix the replaced board. I constantly repair computers through the week and the price is very reasonable. Some various parts that are repaired are on board speakers, memory through its slots, and diagnostics of noise from the fans to adjust the sound to the most possible. What the customers get is the fans not vibrating the cabinent and the cabinent as insulated. When the computers are running, there are several fans that must be working. The first fan that sits on the heat sink, the third is the additional rear fans by the plugs connectors and the front fan by the disk, disc and usb jacks. If the processor fan is not working it can get heated. If the cooling fans are not working they must be repaired to keep from damage by heat and potential hazards. When installing disk drives the choices are usually master, slave, cable select.

The hard drives normally on master and disk drives and removable media are set to cable select. The hard disk may also be on cable selection. The cables used for hard disk, disk drives, disc drives and removable media are typically ide and sata. These cables become bad and need replaced by technicians, when the drives do not appear available for usage. The screen cable is also commonly repaired in displays for proper gui. When discussing about internet connections, the ethernet, and phone jack are two ports that are setup with software from network providers. There are many programs that have the capability to observe the brand and model and place drivers for video, data, chip set, removable media, audio, data, chip set, removable media, audio, networking, and adapters for graphics and performance. The ethernet typically automatically recognizes the data and can readily access the internet. Many modems and wireless networks require drivers and software. Wireless features and many hot keys are setup by the drivers and their install wizard from the computer manufacture. Customers may need to locate drivers on the internet. When newer versions of the drivers are released they may need to be updated in the statistical tag about the drivers. When updating the drivers make sure to restart the computer. This will configure the changes to the computer and make the settings on the machine as current as possible. When error screens appear and the computer seems not to respond, if the programs cannot be resolved by repair or fresh install, the entire computer may need restore of the operating software and all the programs. Many users backup their music, video, and work files from the computer. This can be done in cloud storage and on removable media like cds, usbs, and writable drives. The backups may also be as zip files which are attached to emails and file hosts to provide a download of the content to a computer. It may be important to clean the chasis and the cabinent of all dirt and debris. Then making sure all plugs and connections are secure, all removable media, disc drives operate, hard disk is running and all fans are working properly. We would begin to align the slots on the lids and lock the lid into place. At this point the power would need to be unplugged and replugged back in. This should reset the buzzer and notification of the cover being removed to service the computer. During the reinitiate the pc and computer should do the following, it should load the hard disk, search for removable media and go to the graphic user interface. It will be during removable media, that it will search for disks, discs, and universal serial bus media to load and it is often the users will get prompted whether or not to install and there are times when the booting menu will need to get retrieved to perform tasks. When installing for a printer or fax, scanner or printer there are many machines to choose from and there are choices of laser printers, dot matrix printers, toner.

Printer and ink jet printers. The results of printing depend on the application and usage requirements. Installing printers are done by installing the software and drivers to the computer in the graphic user interface. Then the computer is powered off and the user will need to find the peripheral print terminal known by LPT, LPT1, LPT2 and securely plug in the cable and fasten it to the printer. I would then need to power on the new computer and the printer. It is easier to power on the new device and then wait to load it and then power the pc to prevent hardware problems. There are many printers, copies, digital cameras, and devices that connect through the universal serial bus and some are usb powered and others by their power supply. The second step is locating the speaker input microphone input and speakers input. These are typically 3.5mm jacks. Each plugs without any additional fastenings to the computer and the speakers, desk microphone, and speakers for digital audio playback. The monitor is an Input/Output device and it connects to the video graphic adapter input. It securely fastens to the chasis by two bolts. It is powered normally by a three prong cable and others use dc adapters, and special cables to connect to the ac power supply. The result is achieved also by connecting to a pc slotted video adapter. By this time the computer should be all plugged up correctly and ready to use. Cables may need adjusting and inspected to make certain there are not; cracks, frays, splits, exposed wires, loose ends. Then if the item needs replaced, the technician can help with locating the cables and parts for the computer. To make discs for playback programs are typically downloaded and used to build the following image to disc and cds or digital video media for playback.

Music files may be saved to removable media like storage controllers for other devices. Earphones may be used through the speakers input or the coordinating earphone plug. Before the user attempts to connect earphones. Make sure the volume is adjusted to prevent damage to audio devices and accessories. The earphones may require inspection to prevent damage to the computer by the wiring. Then the earphones and speakers are connected to the computer. When storing a computer for long periods of time, this can be achieved by removing all discs and diskettes from the removable drives and by powering off the computer and removing the power cable from the ac outlet and the rear of the computer chasis.

They can be stored for about a year. After this time the computer may require inspection, cleaning, and replacement of the button cell battery that stores settings and the year, date and time to the cpu. The customers may decide to use dust and dirt cover bags to place on the machine to prevent the accumulation on the inside of the computer. The service the computer for weather damage with an exception to water damage, a technician should be sought to back up data, and determine whether parts can be repair or recycled. The final topic is about servicing the SMPS Serial Mounted Power Supply. This is done by removing the bolts on the power supply and disconnecting the cables to the cpu boards using the flags or pulls to remove a long rectangle connection, a square connection and prong connectors from diskette drives, hard disk, removable drives and the disc drives. Then by removing the switching mounting power supply through the inside of the computer by sliding it off its inserts, the putting the replacement SMPS into position. The user would then connect the rectangle, square and then plug up the prongs. When the user powers on the computer the computer should power on. Other problems maybe in the wires to the cpu and the switches.

By plugging in the rectangle and square wires and plugging the power supply up to the ac outlet, the result is that when powered on and the optional rear switch in the correct position, the computers should power on and off. This will conclude the tutorials and guide for hardware inspection, repair and terminology for computers. When the CPU needs to changed on the desktop, tower, notebook, and laptop, it can be the most difficult and time consuming task. The first thing to do will be to gather my parts or guides needed to do the work. Then we would begin by making the computer powered off and unplugged. Some reasons we would need to change the cpu are the video and onboard audio do not function, the cpu does not turn on, it does not boot, it does not load to system menus and configuration. I would need to press the power button and drain excess energy and I have read that some technicians use a few alligator clips to ground the unit with either a normal grounding or european ground. This grounding has been researched to safely allow the flow of energy from the computer to the floor and can be typically connected to a metal surface to conduct all the energy that continues to flow from the computer.

The user and technician would remove the covers from the chasis and can wipe out any dirt and debris inside on the chasis. The next idea would be to gather tools like a drill, hand driver such as phillips, and the slot driver. If needed a small drip plier to help pull on the plugs that have flags or do not. The flags are like handles and they can be used to remove plugs and re connect each plug. The correct skill is needed, because if the flag breaks it is possible to damage the plug by breaking the connector it has. Then the technician would need to locate a replacement cable at the shop. As a technician I sometimes break cables that are the ribbon for a keyboard, sometimes the cables for devices. Any how the tech will get the idea, sometimes the part has to be ordered, otherwise the wait can be a few days to several weeks. Typically a tech will need more then one screw driver and the bits are varieties of sizes and can be ordered online and in stores.

If the customer breaks a flag on the cables it will not damage the plug but it can be placed into the plug connection and when the keyboard ribbon flag breaks, it may not plug into the connector and may have to be replaced. In the situation where the plug cannot be refitted into the connector by pulling the flap inward or outward and re applying the ribbon down into the plug and closing to secure it into place with the flap that has been provided. When the plug or flap breaks it may need to be glued into place to secure it may need to be glued into place to secure it. When shopping for keyboards, customers may find that there is a lighted option, which allows the keyboard to have an optional back light to view the keys in a well lit method.. These keyboards operate on the power supply of computer. When the keyboards have missing keys, they can be ordered online. When the keyboard has sticky keys or is dirty, it can be cleaned with an air compressed can and can be sanitized with cleaning towels and proper cleaning products.

Many computers utilize several usb parts which can be used to plug in electronics and cables to connect audio and visual devices. There are options to connect items to charge on the ports and it can be used to connect lamps, microphones, earphones, audio devices, cameras, recording devices, telephones, and many electronics. If the usb jack do not work, the user or technician may need to install or update drivers to make the jacks work correctly with the computer. There are many different kinds of usb ports there are 2.0 and high speed ports and always the option for a usb power hub which provides an outlet strip of ports that plug in with an ac adapter and connect to the usb ports. The performance of a power hub is that when putting the drivers for the computer the hub can be much faster. This sorts that data can be copied and data can be sent through the usb much quicker and the devices have quicker responses for gaming and every day tasks, that require fast ports and hubs. Many computers on the cpu have the following, a video feature, sound feature and processor. In various reading, the video feature is used for making the graphic user interface that is seen on displays such as the slot which has a similar role but is different from the factory video features. The sound feature is an impressive digital audio and recording program which is comprised of, head phone jacks, right speaker, left speaker, and the microphone jack. Each of the jacks are 3.5mm in size and there are optional cables known as the patch cable which connect both parts of the audio and recording software. When each part is installed properly, the result is the following, digital audio that is managed using the graphical user Interface. When the software does not function correctly it may require user manual guide or troubleshooting to find the problem in the audio drivers. When users and technicians install their operating systems, they need to update or complete a driver install program that puts devices for printers, scanners, and audio, video, and wifi programs, and wireless controllers. Many computers are manufactured from all around the world, and can be upgraded and downgraded at dealers in your city. Many techs can assist users and dealers in finding what is needed and which is got the performance and workmanship necessary to fulfill the duties of the job.

Which is why Niplaius Computers has came to reason of the concept of a computer cpu where the chassis, power supply, cpu, processor, video, audio, memory and all the jacks and drives which include the hard drive are made of and out of spider web compound. This compound makes almost all of each component friction less and very cool in temperature almost all of the time. This creates the most fabulous and ultra designed computers. In the electric and mechanic object, it makes an experience that is to an aero space realm. Performance like no Computers are made from, where then is much heat, the computers are too slow for operating because too much work is used on the fans to cool the computer to a usable position. When a computer is heated all the time and the fans seem to be running all the time to cool the computer, it may be time to clean the fans and use air can to spray the heat sink to remove all the accumulated dust and dirt. Then the computer should begin to run more within performance and not requiring all of the cooling and exhaust fans. Thus the fans that should be working are the heat sink CPU fan and power supply fan and heavy exhaust is not desired because there may be problems in the cooling of the computer cpu. If the power supply for Switching Mounting Power Supply and the CPU heat sink fan are not on the computer will need to be shut down to prevent damage. The damage that can result can make the computer unoperable for future use. Most computers require proper cooling to operate. The damage can require repair or troubleshooting from a technician. It can be of great advice to have computers serviced as often as needed to keep them in great working condition. Damaged chassis can also be repaired or replaced. Hardware problems like blur or fuzz in the video jack may be fixed by changing its cables and or placing the alternative video jack inside. Keyboard problems can be repaired by driver and reset of the cpu. The mouse may be repaired by cleaning the ball, adjusting the pad, wiping down the surface. Reset the CPU when needed to correct any mouse problems. There are times that the mouse, keyboard and devices do not initialize to repair this, begin by resetting the bios and resetting the smpc and beginning a new session.

When purchasing your computer the things to consider are the following; processing speed, processor, memory and hard disk storage space. Internet wired or WLAN. Then of course the operating technology. Second will be the display, third the type of keyboard and mouse, then the printing and devices. Next gaming stuff and internet software. Additional options; speakers, microphones, disc drives, and removable disk drives. The crazy things that can include would be perform clusters for proccessor, memory, disk space, and internet speed. Analog and digital clusters are all the rage. Important to note that very old computers may require upgrades to be speed driven for the internet. Very old computers have slower processors and less work desk memory, which makes it almost impossible to get all the work done in a quick manner. The old hardware also does not have the storage space of many newer computers. They tend to also not contain the storage media necessary for writing data to newer methods of technologies. Older machines tend to have older software and drives that need to be replaced and updated with newer programs because they begin to be incompatible with newer software products but newer computers can run older products if they specify run in compatibility mode for such operating system.

Also computers may not be compatible with century changes, system dates, battery and hardware settings. Dilometre refered to as storage is quite often important because when I assemble computers I try to not build them from too many recycled parts. The computers built from recycled parts tend to label as recycled. It may be frowned upon because the customers are not buying a used computer but a recycled computer. The correct idea would be a used computer made from recycled components. Typically each part may be greased and oiled to silent unpleasant squeaks and electric noise from within the drives and fans of the chassis. Typically technicians may warranty computers for about 20 days.

Dilometre would like to recommend each computer is placed upright and desktops are stacked on each other there is a difference because the towers are vertical and the desktops lay flat. Never stack them beyond seven high and it is alright to stack in rows. It is good to print a specifications page for each machine for the assistance of resale. Discs that are stuck in the cdrom drive may be removed by using the pin slot on the front and having the disc come out or pull the tray out to remove the media and close the tray to prepare for removal of the disc drive and replacement by a technician. Many new computers require a dvdrom drive to load data and programs. The drive typically supports larger capacity media. Older media may be replaced by the distributor and companies of the program discs, disks,, and diskettes. Many users encourage people to look for new versions of programs for their computers. Many of the operating systems will work on your computer but some require loading to a hard disk and some can be ran from the removable drives like DVD, CD, and removable storage devices. The typical installation usually involves the following load of the installation media, format, selection, partition adjustment, and attempting to setup and initiate the install of programs and applicable programs. The concluding part is boot sequence of the cpu, and registration of the products to the customer. This can be difficult because it may have to be installed many times. When doing this it may not go into the drive because of write errors in hardware and errors in prep for the files and programs. It is important to use the appropriate system discs for each brand of computers and mobile electronic phones. Most discs released by the manufactory of each brand has placed particular builds for every computer. The problem is that the wrong disc means the wrong compatibility and it may result in hardware conflicts and not valid or approved builds. Many brands are strict that the software meets hardware compatibility. It can be frowned upon to use not approved software and drivers. However when it comes to the parts, it is alright to use different brands and products.

Many software programs will inform the install compatibility and what is required. The programs also discuss agreement terms, privacy and any revisions to the programs. Many programs have the option to install older and new versions of each program. How to install programs for the internet. When setting up internet modems, the user begins by plugging in the cable for telephone, and either a usb cable or ethernet plug from the modem to the computer. However before connecting to the computer, the customer needs to install the install the installation disc from the manufacture. Complete the install, then install or update the usb or ethernet driver if needed. Then the computer needs to re begin the boot sequence. This is completed with the internet modem plugged in and ready to connect to the computer by steady and active link blinking on the modem. There are programs that can assist in troubleshooting most troubleshooting problems with the internet connection and the computer. It may require technician work to successfully get the modern to communicate with the web provider and the configuration data to be setup for the computer. The disc drives on computers may be upgraded or downgraded by technicians. This is done by purchasing a drive that has the compatible interface Sata, ide, and cables. For many computers it is possible to connect electronic lamps inside them for impressive performance. Many computers have the option to connect pc slots and they can support fax modems, ethernet modem, gaming adapters, audio adapters, and recording adapters. They have to be analyzed to determine if they fit in the slots. There are normally atleast two slots and up to six for placing the pc adapters. The great news one to two of them are positioned differently and the other slots are for the pc adapters. The processor can be make different if the socket and model are compatible. There will be some hand drivers needed and vinyl or rubber gloves to adjust the bolt to remove the cpu and to place the cpu by aligning the arrow on the side of the cpu and closing the bolt and connecting the smpc to the ac outlet. Then when power is applied the computer should load and in menus the cpu should be showable. The clock speed, model, version, and processes. If the cpu does not fit to the socket it may not work for that computer. Emails are sent through email clients but can be configured to use a mail client on a computer.

Emails can be sent anywhere in the world. Web browsers can be configured by installing them and also determining which one is going to be the default web browser. The computer may require a security center to help manage the experience on the web. Typically anti virus, and malware protection and quarantine repair features and programs. The firewall program can be used to filter programs and connections to prevent malware and malicious and unpleasant programs from affecting computer experiences or interrupting services and programs.

The next topic is about cleaning up a computer to make the performance more great. The task of cleaning computers is to make certain that more storage space can be made and memory can be improved. If the computer cannot be cleaned, programs may have to uninstalled. To make sure there is enough memory, close any open windows, applications that are running on the memory and suspend any security management programs. Then the computer can be scanned for problems and it can be cleaned and optimized. Programs may need to be opened and adjusted for startup so they do not all begin at once. The user may begin by cleaning the junk files on the computer. Then by defragmenting the disk drive to resort the data to improve optimization. There are many kinds of web browsers and typically the include, file, edit, bookmarks, about, settings, and extensions. Each browser has been designed to work by doing a common task, retrieving site pages from the World Wide Web. The pages are then loaded and the coding language is read to make the layout and view possible. The each page is played and can be surfed. It would be a special episode of special hospital where generally Vivian would. Spend much of her time as a celebrity on the show but would run many of the apartments in North Hollywood and Tujunga. Vivian would star in it all the time and she would have the play roles that everyone would dream of she would have a personality that was great and many times she looked great. As a doctor I spend about 20 to 30 minutes with my clients and many of my clients get the results and experience good times with me, because I try to get my clients to focus on nature, the animals, the wildlife and technology. That is some of the reason I write and visit many of my clients. Each client gets introduced to reading material and much of my material is readable by the handicapped or visually impaired.

I provide reference guides and plans to improve my clients futures, especially when I feel things may work for them but I do not participate in those things. These materials are part of the doctors program for clients. They are typically in english language but may be read in any language necessary including tect to speech approved programs and translation guides. In this following tutorial I would like to discuss about typing documents, storing customer information, working with view files and preparing presentations and finally building a resume. Many documents from a few pages to a few hundred pages to several thousand pages are typed in some kind of editor or notepad program.

There are times they require templates to specify in scale the pages, otherwise when using the word wrap all the text can be typed and saved to the computer and printed using an install compatible, driver induced printer. Customer information and address, phone #, email and social media pages can be stored in data sheets. These typically have rows and columns that allow data to be inputed in rows beneath the columns. The columns usually define what will be in the rows below the columns. The data sheets can be stored on the computer and can be printed and emailed. They are usually managed by both offline and online spreadsheet editors. Many businesses require presentations that are shown to the other colleagues. They are done in a presentation making program. That can make slides and let users place headers, text, photos, videos, images and content on the slides for the customers. The presentations can be viewed and they can be printed for notes to follow along with. They can also be emailed. There are features for background effects, gradient fills by many angles horizontal, vertical, polka dot, etc. There is a text options to make both ordered lists and unordered lists. The options of either bullets or numbered lists for text and wrap options for text, and fonts and text options.

Next many of the programs have the same functionality as the presentation program and text typing programs. The resume is a very important document and there are many styles to this and some people prefer to have these made in professional design studios. The plan is simple for the design and I will begin by discussing that this be done in a notepad or text program that has colored text and functions you need for the work. I begin by placing the name on the centered text on the page and strike enter on the keyboard and enter my content information. Then I begin to press enter twice and realign my text to the left of the margin and type all my text for the about section. Then I begin to strike enter and type about my qualifications, degrees, accolades and schooling. Strike enter again and add the names and phone numbers for my references.

The result is a one to two page resume that is ready for my potential employer and it can be saved, printed, and emailed to be provided when needed. This concludes the resume and in a few tips I would like to suggest the customer refrains from using "you" as a referral term. It becomes rude to the customers and they can feel un-satisfied with work provided. It has been concluded that the customers leave the business people and get education from other places. I would learn about this while I was in school in high school. As a doctor I like to promote character building, respect and punctualness. I also like my customers to be trustworthy. I have been a doctor for 3 years now. I work in marketing and my audiences are hopefully thrilled with my work. I also work in marketing and my audiences are hopefully thrilled with my work. I also work as an design artist and repair electronics for customers.

Many of the features and how to work on the programs can be found in the help sections of the programs can be found in the help sections of the programs and can be found in the support communities online. Many technicans are also skilled and the support groups to answer any how to questions on programs for computers. It may help to read the operating unit manual before working with programs and to also review all liscense agreements, terms of service, and privacy policies for all programs and necessary work items. The customer may also decide to visit a librarian or support agent to help resolve their experience with programs. The carat and the mouse pointer are important to learn and also how to move the mouse cursor on the display to properly move, open, drag, stretch, shrink and adjust the properties, features and support of applications. The idea is when customers get the mastery of working with the computer, they will not have much more difficulty in programs. This will conclude the lectures and tutorials for this novel. If the customer has not tried any of the computer guides and books written by me, hopefully they take the opportunity to do so.